Order this book online at www.trafford.com
or email orders@trafford.com

Most Trafford titles are also available at major online book retailers.

 www.trafford.com

North America & international
toll-free: 1 888 232 4444 (USA & Canada)
fax: 812 355 4082

Our mission is to efficiently provide the world's finest, most
comprehensive book publishing service, enabling every author to
experience success. To find out how to publish your book, your way,
and have it available worldwide, visit us online at www.trafford.com

Because of the dynamic nature of the Internet, any web addresses or
links contained in this book may have changed since publication and
may no longer be valid. The views expressed in this work are solely those
of the author and do not necessarily reflect the views of the publisher,
and the publisher hereby disclaims any responsibility for them.

ISBN: 978-1-4251-5023-5 (sc)

Print information available on the last page.

Trafford rev.02/28/2020

To Alfie

A very large family
Lives in a house
With six dogs inside!
It's no place for a mouse.

Each one has their story,
Which happened before.
They used to be street dogs,
But not anymore.

The first one is Alfie,
A pink Shar Pei.
He was found in the street;
He was running away.

His owners were mean;
They'd hit him and scream.
But Alfie escaped
And found his new fate.

Now he lives like a king
And snores like a pig
While asleep in his bed,
Which is so soft and big.

He loves to sunbathe
And pee on the flowers.
He never smells bad,
Although he hates showers.

He tends to be fat,
So his diet is lean.
But his food sure is tasty;
It's Royal cuisine.

Irresponsible owners
Bought her one day,
But when they got bored,
They gave her away.

The very large family
Brought Petus home.
They knew if they didn't
She'd end up alone.

This hungry white poodle
Is so very loud!
She barks for food
Day in and day out.

She's eighteen years old,
The queen of the crowd,
She can't be bothered;
She's peevish and proud.

She makes dinners awkward
With her whining concerts;
She ought to be censored,
But here she's just pampered.

Lola's a Poodle,
A long-tailed redhead.
She's happy, she's pretty,
And very well fed.

Eight years have gone by
Since she was saved just in time
From being hit by a car
The day her life changed by far.

She looked like a mop,
She's sure changed a lot.
Now she looks like a princess
And smells better than incense.

She's both agile and fragile,
So girly and gracious.
You'll never come by
A dog that's more precious.

A dog shelter needed
People who cared
About lost, lonely dogs;
There were too many there.

The very large family
Drove out to see
The cute little doggies.
Which would it be?

The cutest Chihuahua
Was brought out to show
To the family members,
Who asked if he'd grow.

He was so very tiny,
His ears looked so big,
His coat really shiny;
He was thin as a twig.

The very large family
Liked him so much,
They took him home;
Now he's part of the
bunch.
His name is Pepis.
He sleeps all day long,
He eats very well,
So he's healthy and strong.

He pees on the walls,
Which are so hard to clean.
It's no use being angry,
It's just his routine.

A Miniature Pinscher
Was let out of a car
By very mean owners
Who didn't live far.

This happened one Sunday
During a storm.
Although it was raining,
The weather was warm.

The very large family
Saw her by luck.
They were driving by slowly
And stopped their truck.

The poor thing was scared,
But now she's okay.
Her name is Yolo
And she's here to stay.

When Barbie was found,
She was very sick;
She had an infection
And needed help quick.

She had an operation;
She was very brave.
It was her salvation.
She was worthy to save.

Her hair was a mess,
She needed a makeover;
The best dog beautician
Was quickly sent over.

Now she and Yolo,
Both one year old,
Play day and night
And mess up the household.

The House of Dogs
Is a kid's dream come true.
A house full of animals,
Is like living in a zoo!

All animals are beautiful,
But the friendliest of all
Are definitely street dogs,
Whether big or small.

Dogs in a pet store
Are always so sad.
They're very expensive,
And that's too bad.

It's easy to find
At the shelter near you
A wonderful dog
Who needs love and care, too.

So adopt a dog;
You could even take two.
It's a lot of fun
And a nice thing to do!

This book of poems
Is dedicated to dogs
Who are no longer with us,
But were loved just as much.

In an ideal world,
They'd still be here,
Shining their light
Which we hold so dear.

They lived happy lives.
Their memory we embrace.
But now they're much better
In a special place.

There's no need to worry,
We'll see them again.
We'll all be together
Someday..... until then.

THANKS

To my Mom and Dad
Who taught me to be
Good to all animals
And gave so much to me.

To my husband whose heart
Is big as can be,
For he always brings home
Dogs from the street.

To my family-in-law
Who are just as kind;
They take care of street dogs,
As many as they find.

To my friends and family
Who are always with me,
Although some may find this
Incredibly crazy.

In memory of Farrah, Doty, Titina,
Titino, Nena, Coco, Muñeco,
Migui, Norka, Pierre, Piersita,
Tosky, Sax, Sasha, Scraps,
Jackie, Kika, Hilaria, Moon,
Rome, Anouck,...

Go to
fb.me/thehouseofdogs.org
to see real photos and videos of
The House of Dogs

Printed in the United States
By Bookmasters